PROCLAIM *and* PRAISE

A Lenten Journey for Abiding in Christ

RALPH DOUGLAS WEST
MINISTRIES

Houston

Proclaim and Praise – A Lenten Journey for Abiding in Christ
Copyright © 2012, 2013, 2014, 2026 by Ralph Douglas West

ISBN: 978-1-7331718-6-1

Ralph Douglas West Ministries
5725 Queenston Blvd.
Houston, TX 77084

Scripture quotations are taken from the Holy Bible, New International Version®, NIV®.

Printed in the United States of America

PROCLAIM *and* PRAISE

A Lenten Journey for Abiding in Christ

RALPH DOUGLAS WEST

THE JOURNEY

- Ash Wednesday through Palm Sunday – Triumphal Entry themes (Day 1 – Day 19)
- Holy Week through Easter – Crucifixion and Resurrection (Days 20 – 25)
- Post-Easter – Resurrection Appearances and Living out the Faith (Days 26 – 40)

CONTENTS

Psalm 96:2-3 (NIV)

Sing to the Lord, praise his name;
proclaim his salvation day after day.
Declare his glory among the nations,
His marvelous deeds among all peoples.

INTRODUCTION

For most of us Christians, Easter comes and goes by so quickly. Indeed, the brightness and excitement associated with this special day are often just a distant memory for the rest of the year. While our church now faithfully observes Holy Week—gathering for Maundy Thursday, Good Friday, and other sacred services—Easter can often feel like a one-day affair in our hearts. We attend the services, but many of us still approach Easter without the deep personal preparation this celebration deserves. Perhaps this is because the solemn, reflective days leading up to Easter, though profound, do not carry the triumphant joy we experience on Easter Sunday.

But what if we could change how we celebrate Easter this year by preparing ourselves in sincere reflection during Lent?

Lent, known in Latin as Quadragesima, meaning fortieth, is a solemn season in the liturgical calendar of many Christian denominations. It begins on Ash Wednesday and spans approximately six weeks, leading up to Easter Sunday. The traditional purpose of Lent is to prepare the believer through prayer, repentance, almsgiving, self-denial, and a renewed focus on Christ. These practices have long been observed by Christians in Anglican, Lutheran, Methodist, Reformed, and Roman Catholic traditions, and some Anabaptist and evangelical churches also embrace them today.

Lent is traditionally described as lasting forty days, reflecting the time Jesus spent fasting in the wilderness before beginning His public ministry, during which He endured the devil's temptation.

Throughout the centuries, Christian communities have observed Lent in different ways. Some denominations provide specific guidelines for fasting, while others view fasting as a private discipline between the believer and the Lord. In many churches today, the Lenten season is also marked by intentionally setting aside everyday distractions. You may have heard someone say, "I gave up something for Lent." Whether it is food, entertainment, or social media, the purpose is the same: to engage.

Although the practices may differ, the goal of Lent remains constant. It is a time to loosen our attachment to the world and refocus our hearts on God and on Christ's sacrifice on the cross.

This devotional book is a forty-day guide designed to help you prepare your heart, mind, and spirit for the joyful celebration of Easter. It also moves beyond personal reflection by inviting you to share the gospel with others. Each devotion includes an exhortation to witness and a prayer you can adapt during your time with the Lord.

This Easter offers us an opportunity to create a day we will always cherish in our spiritual memories, rather than letting the day's significance fade in the weeks and months that follow. The resurrection of Jesus Christ signifies the promise of eternal life with Him, which is a compelling reason to worship Him sincerely and wholeheartedly.

DAY 1

Are You in the Picture?

For we are God's masterpiece. He has created us anew in Christ Jesus, so we can do the good things he planned for us long ago.
Ephesians 2:10 NLT

In March of 1990, two men posing as Boston police officers entered the Boston Isabella Stewart Gardner Museum, tied up the night watchman, and pilfered thirteen masterpieces painted by artists like Rembrandt, Manet, Degas, and Johannes Vermeer. It has been identified as the largest art heist in history. At that time, the art was valued at $500 million. If you visited the art museum at that time, you would have seen empty frames where those fine masterpieces once hung. While touring that very room where those famous portraits were displayed, I could not resist the urge to put my face in the big, empty frame. The first thing I wanted to know was this: Do I look good in that frame?

The Gospel of Luke gives a colorful account of Jesus' Triumphal Entry into Jerusalem and the anonymous people who participated in both the prearrangements and the moment when crowds waved palm branches and shouted "Hosanna!" as Jesus rode a donkey into the city. Luke tells the story from different angles, showing Jesus, the disciples, and the nameless people in the crowd. But today, it is as if Luke is saying as he holds up an empty frame, asking, "Do you fit into this picture? Do you belong here with Jesus?"

Ephesians 2:10 teaches us that we are God's masterpiece, created to display salvation, service, commitment, and compassion. You were designed to fit perfectly into His frame. But like thieves who break into a museum and steal priceless works of art, the enemy of our souls broke in and pulled us from our rightful place, seeking to destroy what God created. Yet through Jesus Christ, God graciously restored you as His glorious masterpiece. Now He says, "As My greatest work, I want you displayed for the world to see—the beauty of a transformed life."

Heavenly Father, though the Enemy stole us from our original picture frames, You have graciously restored us as Your glorious masterpieces. While we are on display for the unsaved world to see, let us reflect the beautiful work of Your hands through our compassion and love for them. Then they can become Your masterpieces of grace as well. In Jesus' name, Amen.

DAY 2

The Lord Needs It

"Go to the village ahead of you, and as you enter it, you will find a colt tied there, which no one has ever ridden. Untie it and bring it here. If anyone asks you, 'Why are you untying it?' say, 'The Lord needs it.'
Luke 19:30-31

From the foundations of the world, everything had been prepared, and now it was set in motion. The convergence of the Old Testament Scriptures had finally come to a head: Now the King is coming. As the journey began, from the Mount of Olives and from Bethphage in Bethany, He would make His way. For the past three years, aside from crossing the Sea of Galilee, the Lake of Gennesaret, the only mode of transportation Jesus used was His two feet in His leather sandals. For the first time, the walking Messiah, the King, would be riding. The Lord needed the disciples to bring Him an unbroken donkey, a colt, ready and waiting for their arrival. The donkey that had never been ridden submitted to the King of Glory, willingly bearing Him on its back—a clear visual demonstration that Jesus is Lord over all creation.

In the same way, Jesus wants you to bring Him something or somebody that He needs. That's where you may fit in the frame. It may be as simple as inviting someone to a church event or donating food to the church pantry. You may say, though, "I don't believe that God is so situated in my life that I would bring anyone to Him or that I would bring something to Him." But perhaps the Lord Jesus wants you to identify with the donkey by taking Him somewhere He needs to go—across the street or across the sea to share His life-changing gospel with those who do not know Him.

REFLECT ON THIS

*"Jesus wants you to bring
Him something or somebody
that He needs."*

Heavenly Father, unlike this submissive donkey colt, we often buck and kick in stubborn resistance against Your will. You often want to ride us where we don't want to go because the path is hard or inconvenient. Forgive us for our selfishness and change our hearts so that we will gladly be Your humble servants to a broken, dying world. In Jesus' name, Amen.

DAY 3

A Donkey?!

They brought it to Jesus, threw their cloaks on the colt, and put Jesus on it.
Luke 19:35

Unlike other noble animals such as lions and eagles, donkeys have never gotten much respect. In fact, some things about donkeys make people laugh—they are stubborn, recalcitrant, and slow. Lions demand respect. Dogs receive affection from their owners. Dolphins are viewed with a kind of curiosity. Eagles are held up as the emblem of the nation, but not a donkey. They don't get much respect. Who wants to be identified with a donkey? Interestingly, the Lord of creation could have selected any animal to bear him on His kingly ride through Jerusalem, yet He asked for a donkey. Why didn't He enter on the back of a white steed prancing majestically down the street? That would have made for a grander entrance.

Perhaps Jesus used a donkey because it's the most unlikely, unusable animal that you would ride down the middle of Main Street leading a parade. It was the Lord's way of saying, "Hey, for those of you who are prejudiced and biased against others because of their race, social standing, or checkered past, you reject them, but not me. I take people just the way they are and use them for what they have been created to be." Perhaps you can take Jesus where He needs to go or take someone else where they need to be to meet Jesus. God has this uncanny way of using unlikely people— He really does, and I'm amazed by how He does it.

REFLECT ON THIS

"God has this uncanny way of using unlikely people—he really does."

Heavenly Father, it never ceases to amaze us how You use the unlikeliest people to accomplish great things for the kingdom of God. In a way, each one of us is like this humble donkey. None of us is worthy to bear the message of the gospel because of what we've done. But the good news is that You can use anyone willing to submit to Your perfect will. We are honored to carry the gospel to everyone we know. In Jesus' name, Amen.

DAY 4

Making the Lord's Ride Smoother

As he went along, people spread their cloaks on the road.
Luke 19:36

Whenever the chivalrous courtier Sir Walter Raleigh attended Her Majesty Elizabeth I and she encountered a waterlogged or muddy road, he would remove his fur coat and lay it on the ground. She then passed ever so nicely, walking on the back of his mink. He would do this because he wanted to make the queen's movements over the rough terrain easy and smooth. During the Triumphal Entry, this is exactly what the people of Jerusalem were doing. They removed their cloaks and spread them on the rough, uneven, damp, filthy road to make the ride smoother for their king, Jesus. It was a gesture of loving respect, marked by humility and submission.

What are you doing in your life, ministry, or work to make it easy for the King to travel? You may have been telling everyone how much you love Jesus, identifying as a Christian by wearing your cross, carrying your Bible, and posting scripture on social media. Yet some of us make Jesus' ride rough when we misrepresent Him in those supposedly private moments at our office, home, school, dormitory, or place of recreation through rude or unkind speech and actions that betray our underlying attitude. Some emit an unpleasant aroma of anger, bitterness, or depression that completely turns off unsaved people. Resolve today to become a loving, merciful, noble courtier of the King, and unsaved people will respond more positively to your witness.

Heavenly Father, we confess that oftentimes we don't make the ride smooth for You. Although we tell our unsaved friends that we love You, our actions and attitude don't match our words. Lord, please cultivate the fruit of the Spirit in our lives so that we will live for You every day of the week, not just on Sunday. In Jesus' name, Amen.

DAY 5

God in the Ordinary

My heart says of you, "Seek his face!" Your face, LORD, I will seek.
Psalm 27:8

Brother Lawrence, a 17th-century Carmelite monk, wrote a life-changing book that thousands of Christians keep on their bookshelves: *Practicing the Presence of God.* Where he learned to meet God was in the kitchen, doing mundane, everyday work—washing dishes. This seemingly routine task was not too small for him, and it did not belittle who he was. There he was, washing dishes while enjoying God's presence. Kathleen Norris, also from the Catholic tradition, wrote a beautiful book titled Quotidian Mysteries: Laundry Liturgy *and Woman's Work.* Its major theme is the intriguing way God breaks through our awareness in ordinary moments.

Indeed, God breaks through and meets you in ordinary times. Some of you would be much more spiritual if you did not think you could decide how, when, and where God was going to show up. Sometimes, a real church can break out at your house or in your car. I am not saying that is how it always happens. You may be taking your daily walk around the neighborhood and start thinking about Jesus and His goodness. Suddenly, you find yourself shedding happy tears as you reflect on how good God has been to you. If your unsaved friends or family see you, do not apologize for those tears. Share with them how God has blessed you!

REFLECT ON THIS

"God breaks through and meets you in ordinary times."

Heavenly Father, at times we wrongly think that You only manifest Your presence to us at church, a Christian conference, a retreat, or some other "godly" setting. But how often we forget that You are omnipresent, and You promised You would never leave nor forsake us. Help us to be more aware of You during the ordinary tasks of daily life. After a while, we will realize that the glory of Your presence will be expressed in our countenance, attitudes, words, and deeds. In Jesus' name, Amen.

DAY 6

Shouting "Hosanna" For All the Miracles

When he came near the place where the road goes down the Mount of Olives, the whole crowd of disciples began joyfully to praise God in loud voices for all the miracles they had seen.
Luke 19:37

The streets are full of people making all kinds of joyful noises and waving their hands, tree branches, and palm leaves. We know what they were saying: "Blessed is the King who comes in the name of the Lord!" Why did they get all excited? For all the miracles they had seen. Someone in the crowd had witnessed Jesus take five loaves of bread and two fish to feed a multitude of five thousand people, with plenty left over. Some of the people there probably witnessed ten lepers—outcasts—become clean. Nine of them forgot to turn around, but one came back and said, "They may have forgotten, but I've come back to say, 'Thank You for cleaning me up and giving me a new start and a new direction.' "The nine probably were not there at the Triumphal Entry, but one of the noisy shouters was probably that healed leper, telling them, 'If you only knew like I know what the Lord had done, you would be shouting in my place."

So, you can nominate whoever you want to be in that crowd. Hopefully, you are in that same grateful bunch when you think of what God has done for you, especially how He has forgiven you and transformed your life. You can get as loud as you want, shouting like those jubilant people lining the streets a couple of thousand years ago, "Hosanna! Blessed be the King who comes in the name of the Lord!"

Heavenly Father, we cannot praise You enough for healing and restoring our lives in every way. We are just as grateful as that one leper out of ten. We can joyfully sing the Christian musician Carman's lyrics: No way, we are not ashamed of the gospel, or His name, Holy hands are lifted high/To the name of Jesus Christ. Let this praise always be in our mouths! In Jesus' name, Amen.

DAY 7

A Banner for Jesus' Row

May we shout for joy over your victory and lift up our banners in the name of our God.
Psalm 20:5

Have you ever been to a basketball game where the fans hold up banners and signs supporting their favorite player? The crowd erupts in cheers, waving their signs high to show their loyalty and support. Many years ago, my buddy got me court-side tickets to the Spurs-Knicks basketball game. I sat next to Tim Duncan's uncle, who was visually impaired and listening to the game on the radio. They had a banner saying, "Go, Tim Duncan!" Now, those of you who know me understand that one thing I do not like to do is hold up a banner. But a consulate from the Virgin Islands enthusiastically asked me to lift it up with him. Because I was on the Duncan row, I was required to hold it up.

That is what the people did for Jesus during the Triumphal Entry: they waved palm branches, shouted praises, and made it clear which side they were on.

Likewise, if you are going to be on Jesus' row, you must hold up the sign: "Go, Jesus, Go!" Make a noise for Him! Now, I'm not suggesting that we all must do it the same way. You don't have to be loud all the time. Some days you feel like standing, and other days you may want to just sit quietly. What

I am saying is that your praise should have some content to it, and here's the reason why: The next time you do not physically feel like praising the Lord, you must look to where the Lord has brought you from, and you cannot help but praise! Clap your hands, stomp your feet, wave your hands, or nod your head—but there should be some expression of praise that says, "Lord, You have been good to me, better to me than I've been to myself."

REFLECT ON THIS

"If you're going to be on
Jesus' row, you must hold up
the sign: 'Go, Jesus, Go!'"

Heavenly Father, we remember how pitiful and wretched our lives were before You found us. We're forever grateful for Your outpouring of gracious love and mercy through the sacrificial death of Your Son, Jesus. Because of Your mighty deliverance, we cannot stay silent. In fact, we ask that You make our very bodies instruments of praise and worship to You. In Jesus' name, Amen.

DAY 8

Praise God with What You Have in Your Hand

. . . others cut branches from the trees and spread them on the road.
Matthew 21:8

The people shouted, "Hosanna!" while waving branches from all kinds of trees—palm, myrtle, willow—whatever they had in their hands. For the same reason, you should have something in your hand that you praise Him with. Are you willing to praise Him with the mind He has given to you? I always appreciate people who are smart enough to know that worshiping God does not diminish one's intellect. In fact, I believe the more intellectual you are, the more you should praise Him.

Sometimes, when we achieve success, whether through education, a good job, or building something meaningful in our lives, we may begin to feel self-sufficient. It is easy to forget that every good thing we have ultimately comes from God's hand. Without realizing it, we can slip into thinking we are doing God a favor by showing up in His house, rather than recognizing that He is the one who gave us the capacity to achieve in the first place. Yet, when challenges arise and we seek refuge in the sanctuary, God graciously allows us to find shelter and reminds us that our accomplishments have never made us self-sufficient. It is His grace that has sustained us all along.

At times, we may hesitate to praise God because we feel we must meet certain criteria or be in a particular spiritual state. This hesitation often causes us to miss opportunities to experience His presence. Some may think, "I would praise Him, but I am not worthy enough," forgetting that none of us is perfect. If we were, we would not need Jesus. We praise Him precisely because we need Him, so let us offer whatever we have in our hands.

When we praise God joyfully, regardless of our circumstances, we not only draw closer to Him but also inspire others to encounter the gospel of Jesus Christ.

Heavenly Father, it seems like every time we think we've got it made through our own abilities and smarts, You allow situations to arise in our lives to show us that we cannot make it on our own. There are other times when we want to praise You, but do not feel we meet nebulous spiritual criteria. For both occasions, remind us to just praise You with whatever is in our hand, and we know that we will end up directly in Your loving arms. In Jesus' name, Amen.

DAY 9

Worship God with Your Gifts

Whatever your hand finds to do, do it with all your might.
Ecclesiastes 9:10

French novelist Anatole France tells a legend about a monk who was not as gifted and talented as all the other monks. He could not draw or do arts and crafts. He could not transcribe. At that very moment, all he had to give to God was his ability to juggle. Feeling inferior and out of place when all the monks went to lunch, prayer time, or choir rehearsal, this monk went inside the chapel and juggled with his feet in front of the statue of Mary—just using the gift he had. When the other monks found out, they admonished him, "You don't do that in here; that doesn't belong here." According to the legend, Mary stepped down from the statue and started wiping her tears with his garments. They had broken her heart by disallowing this monk to use the only thing he knew how to do.

God may never ask you to be a scholar, theologian, historian, or linguist. Instead, He asks you to do what He has created you to do, so you should praise Him with whatever He has gifted you. If you have a hammer, hammer out justice and evil; if you have a voice, lift it up in praise to Him; if you have a pen, write to His glory and honor. Whatever gifts and talents you have, use them for the *glory* of God.

Heavenly Father, we realize now that praise and worship do not consist only of singing and clapping in Sunday morning services. Instead, You have called us to worship You daily with the gifts and talents that You have so generously bestowed upon us. Help us to serve You with all our mind, strength, and soul. You have given us Your all through Your Son, so we should do no less. In Jesus' name, Amen.

DAY 10

"It Does Not Take All of That"

*Some of the Pharisees in the crowd said to Jesus,
"Teacher, rebuke your disciples!"*
Luke 19:39

Even today, there are always those who feel uncomfortable with exuberant worship, saying, "Jesus, tell the people to be quiet. Tone it down; this is church." Perhaps they have advanced degrees and successful careers. Perhaps they live in comfortable neighborhoods and value order and decorum in worship. They may prefer to control the services rather than allow the Holy Spirit to move freely. So, they cross their arms, frown, and refrain from joining in joyful praise and worship, thinking to themselves, "It does not take all that." The good news is that education, culture, and genuine celebration can coexist beautifully in worship.

Some time ago, I was hosting a group of around twenty doctoral candidates from United Seminary in Ohio. They asked me, "Do you still celebrate the Lord with exuberant praise and worship?" One of the young students told me there was no place for it because "it was old-timey and out of the way." I replied, "You can believe anything you want, but I take it that you don't pastor yet." He said, "No." I said, "Well. When you do, you will understand. You see, when people have been

32

going through difficult times all week, they want to believe in a Jesus who will get them out. That's celebration time."

Listen, if you want your Jesus to stay locked in a grave, I am not upset with you for believing that way, but my Jesus got up. If I do not cry out, the rocks will.

REFLECT ON THIS

"My Jesus got up. If I do not cry out, the rocks will."

Heavenly Father, we refuse to be intimidated by those who would try to restrain our joyful praise or dampen our enthusiasm in worship. Instead, we just want to praise You all the more because heartfelt worship is never out of fashion in Your eyes. We rejoice in You! Praise Your holy name, forever and ever! In Jesus' name, Amen.

DAY 11

Rocks Do Talk

"I tell you," he replied, "if they keep quiet, the stones will cry out."
Luke 19:40

Scientists have discovered that rocks produce sound. Seismologists who study earthquakes have found that before an earthquake occurs, rocks begin to "talk," speaking their own language as the earth's tectonic plates shift and create pressure. Some witnesses describe it as a rumbling sound, like distant thunder or wind approaching. One said it sounded like a cannon breaking in the distance. The rocks are literally crying out before the ground shakes.

Jesus knew this scientific truth when He said, "If these people keep quiet, the stones will cry out." Rocks will talk. In other words, if you do not shout, God has a whole creation that will praise Him. Creation is always in harmony with itself. There are thousands of universes singing God's praises right now, billions of galaxies lifting their voices in an orchestra. All of God's nature joins together in a chorus, singing the song of creation that God still lives and reigns. God still rules.

Will you be in harmony with creation? When creation sings, will you join in and get in tune? You may break the harmony, but God has a way of calling creation to join the celebration—even the rocks will cry out if we do not. I do not want a rock to stand up and talk about how good God has been, because I know for myself what the Lord has done for me.

REFLECT ON THIS

*God has a whole creation
that will praise Him — with or
without you.*

Heavenly Father, every time we look at Your marvelous creation, we observe the various ways it praises and worships You. The trees of the field clap their hands, and their very leaves whisper Your name. The rocks cry out before an earthquake. The thunder that rolls declares Your might and majesty. As Your redeemed creation, we have lips, hands, feet, and minds to praise You with. We gladly join in tune with all the universe in giving You praise, for You are worthy! In Jesus' name, Amen.

DAY 12

How God Uses Rocks

"Strike the rock, and water will come out of it for the people to drink."
Exodus 17:6

I can name two or three rocks that once spoke and still speak to us today. There is an *unapproachable* rock. In Exodus 19, Moses climbs up to that rock—a rock filled with fire and smoke, a rock that is awesome, dangerous, and unapproachable. It is a rock on which God gave him a law that we still hold in our hands today. When careless worshippers tried to tread upon that stone and touched it, they fell down dead, warning us that you do not play with holiness. You must reverence it and then get out of the way.

What about the *rock of provision*? In Exodus 17, after the children of Israel had been emancipated from Egyptian slavery and were walking through the wilderness to the Promised Land, these cattle drivers and herdsmen became concerned that there may not be enough water, not just to slake their thirst but to keep their livestock alive. They started complaining, "Moses, you brought us out here to die of thirst in the desert," and God said, "Do not let them panic. Do not let them pass out. Stop by the rock and speak to it." When Moses spoke, water gushed from the rock, demonstrating that He is water in dry places, both then and now. He is life where there is death. He is the one who can replenish us when our lives seem so empty. We can tell others that if they place their trust in God, He can be their rock of provision, too.

Heavenly Father, we take comfort in knowing that You are both the unapproachable rock and the rock of provision— holiness and mercy combined. Today, we come before You with reverence and awe to humbly seek Your providential mercy for our lives. We thank You that because of the new covenant in Christ Jesus, we can come boldly (not arrogantly) into Your presence as Your redeemed children. In Jesus' name, Amen.

DAY 13

Out of the Mouths of Babes

and said to Him, "Do You hear what these are saying?"
And Jesus said to them, "Yes. Have you never read,
'Out of the mouth of babes and nursing infants
You have perfected praise'?"
Matthew 21:16 (NKJV)

The children started crying out, "Hosanna!" But the Pharisees were just trying to shut them up: "Shh... be quiet. Go back to that student center. That's what they built it for. Don't come over here." The children did not really know what they were saying. They had heard what the parents were saying, and so they started shouting, "Hosanna!" But the Pharisees nervously told them, "Shh... be quiet. You're too loud. It doesn't take all of that in church." The children kept crying out, "Hosanna in the highest!" The religious leaders got angry: "Shh . . .We're going to put all of you, little ragamuffins, out of here. Go away!"

When Jesus heard the religionists say, "Get those children out!" He promptly replied, "Leave those children alone," and quoted Psalm 8:2 to underline His rebuke.

During that particular day and age, children were supposed to be "seen but not heard." On two previous occasions when parents brought their children to Jesus for a blessing, the disciples tried to send them away, probably because they thought the children would "bother" Him. But instead, Jesus welcomed the children, saying, "Let the children come unto Me, for such is the kingdom of heaven." In other words, children have essential qualities for citizens in the heavenly city: they are honest and humble, unafraid to express what is truly in their hearts. As Christians, we should allow this same childlikeness to permeate our very being—in our worship, work, and witness.

REFLECT ON THIS

"Children are honest and humble, unafraid to express what is truly in their hearts."

Heavenly Father, we long to be like little children in Your presence—not just in church, but in every moment of our lives. Reveal to us the places in our spirits, minds, and emotions where we have grown hardened or resistant. Set us free from the chains of legalistic religion, and teach us to worship You with passionate, childlike abandon. In Jesus' name, Amen.

DAY 14

The Right Praise at the Wrong Time

"As the heavens are higher than the earth, so are my ways higher than your ways and my thoughts than your thoughts."
Isaiah 55:9

How many times have people made affirmations that are proven to be hilariously ridiculous and wrong? Consider some of the greatest misstatements in all world history. Western Union in 1876 sent a memo out that read, "The telephone has too many shortcomings to be seriously considered as a means of communication. This device is inherently of no value." Movie buffs may remember this line: "I'm just glad it'll be Clark Gable who falls on his face and not Gary Cooper." Those were the critics' words when Cooper rejected the leading role in *Gone with the Wind*. In 1962, Decca Records rejected a young rock band with this dismissive comment: "We don't like their sound, and the guitar is on its way out," turning down The Beatles.

These are statements made about the right thing at the wrong time. When Romans by the roadside saw Jesus riding a donkey during the Triumphal Entry, they giggled and snickered under their breath because they had been part of such events for so many years. "What a strange parade! What an awkward-looking king! He has no crown. His soldiers have no swords. Is this supposed to be what is going to threaten the kingdom of Rome? Is this what's going to upset our government?" Likewise, when you share the gospel with others, you may get the same scornful reaction. But do not let that stop you. Instead, tell them your testimony. They cannot sneer at the way the Lord has transformed your life.

Heavenly Father, the people in Jesus' day did not understand His kingdom, and today they still don't understand. They scornfully mock a meek and mild Jesus who teaches forgiveness rather than revenge, selflessness rather than selfishness, and humility rather than self-promotion. As His followers, we also will be understood when we practice His ways. Give us the grace and courage to live for You in the face of scorn and ridicule. When they realize their approach does not work, they will come to us for answers. In Jesus' name, Amen.

DAY 15

Save Us, Lord, NOW!

LORD, save us! LORD, grant us success! Blessed is he who comes in the name of the LORD. From the house of the LORD we bless you.
Psalm 118:25-27

"Hosanna, Hosanna!" What they were really shouting was, "Save us, Lord, now! Give us power now. Give us precedence now. Give us preeminence now at last, Lord. Make us better than the Romans. Come on!" The zealots were waiting around the corner, sharpening their daggers, anticipating this new nationalist movement to strike out against the Romans. They were poised to upset the established order—they only needed one sign or signal to set everything in motion.

Amidst all that electricity, it boils down to this: They were asking Jesus to do what He could not do from the back of a donkey—to improve their lives and give them a makeover. It is no different today. With many of us evangelical Christians, what we want is a cross-less Christianity. We tell Jesus, "Just give me a makeover. Make me feel better about myself. Retouch the photographs of my life." On the back of a donkey, all Jesus can do is give us some good advice. The only one who could save us had to go to the cross, and all of us could stand a little more saving from our limitations, from our mistakes. We should rather ask Jesus, "Save me from my habits, my addictions, and my problems. Save me from my burdens and missteps. Save me from my critical judgment. Save me from my own hypocrisy. Save me now, Lord!"

Heavenly Father, we are dissatisfied with the watered-down gospel that teaches us to seek self-fulfillment and prosperity for our lives. Instead, we want the true gospel of salvation— the Christianity that saves us from our self-centered behaviors and transforms us into who You want us to be. Indeed, our hope is built on nothing less than Jesus' blood and righteousness. In Jesus' name, Amen.

DAY 16

Our Unpredictable God

*"Who is this that obscures my plans with words
without knowledge?"*
Job 38:2

The Triumphal Entry shatters our notion regarding the predictability of God. Jesus' final arrival into Jerusalem would be spent on the back of this donkey instead of a steed, dressed in desert garb rather than regal finery. Rather than ascending to a human throne of majesty, He comes to the throne of the cross. This humble entrance demonstrates that God still disrupts our equilibrium. He does not play the game of life the way we expect Him to.

I appreciate the unpredictability of our Lord, and that is what the season of Lent and Easter reminds us—that God cannot be predicted. You cannot nail God down or tame Him. Just when you think you have figured God out, He does something completely different. You cannot hem Him in or place Him in a box. No wonder people in that ancient time rejected Jesus: He was unpredictable. Jesus definitely did not do what was expected of an earthly king.

By definition, God is able, and He has revealed this in both the biblical record and our lives that HE IS ABLE. He may not choose to do things the way we typically want Him to, but God does not have to do what we want because He is the sovereign Lord of all. When our unsaved friends and family express bewilderment about current events—when life seems chaotic and unpredictable—we can assure them that the Lord is in control, even when his ways surprise us.

Heavenly Father, we may not understand Your ways or predict how You're going to move, but there is one thing we do know: You are the good and just God, so we can trust You in all things. This is our assurance and hope. Increase our faith as we walk with You daily so that we will obey You without question, even if we do not understand why or how. In Jesus' name, Amen.

DAY 17

Jesus Conquers Through Love

Love never fails.
1 Corinthians 13:8

Napoleon Bonaparte once said, "Charlemagne, seas and all, will be gone, and we conquered worlds by force. Jesus did it by love, and He's loved and remembered by millions. We struck fear into the hearts of the people that we served. Our names will be lost in oblivion, and this Lord came with no sword or shield, and no machinery, just with the object of love." Even this great emperor had to acknowledge the life-giving power of Jesus' love for the world.

Although other kings conquer by military might, Jesus says, "I'm going to conquer people with love." Today, billions of us gather in church each Sunday, reverencing Him for what He has done. He did not coerce us into worshiping Him; instead, He demonstrated His love for us by dying on the cross to free us from our chains of sin. As His followers, we also should share His love with a spiritually dead world through acts of kindness and mercy. Instead of beating them over the head with a Bible, we must take the time to simply *love* people. Remember, they will not care until we show them how much we care.

Who in your life needs to experience the conquering love of Jesus Christ through you this week? Is it a challenging family member, a difficult coworker, or maybe a stranger you encounter on a regular basis? How might you demonstrate His love through a specific act of kindness or mercy rather than words alone?

REFLECT ON THIS

"They will not care until we show them how much we care."

Heavenly Father, Your dear Son Jesus conquered the world both then and now through His mighty love. We cannot begin to comprehend its depth, height, and breadth, but we desire to love others into the kingdom despite our limited understanding. Teach us to love others with Your glorious agape love—a love that is compassionate, forgiving, and kind. In Jesus' name, Amen.

DAY 18

God's Kind of Blessings

May God bless us still so that all the ends of the earth will fear him.
Psalm 67:7

Even in that unpredictability, God still blesses—just not the way you think. Many people have scratched and clawed through life without experiencing material prosperity, yet they remain highly faithful to God. In Genesis 12, God promised Abraham that He would bless him with so many descendants that he would not be able to count them. It was only after a generation had passed that God fulfilled that promise. Once the promise was given in the form of his firstborn son, God told Abraham to sacrifice him on a mountain. Later, God provided a ram for the sacrifice. Joseph saved Egypt from a dire famine; however, he was first sold into slavery by his brothers and spent time in prison before reaching the pinnacle of the palace. David, a man after God's own heart, would ascend to the throne—not until he had made moral missteps and experienced his own children turning their backs on him.

Indeed, God *moves* in mysterious ways, His wonders to perform. We often selfishly want to be blessed so that we can enjoy life, but God has a larger goal for blessing us. Regarding Abraham, Joseph, and David, He blessed them so the entire world would know Him, and in turn, be blessed themselves. Of course, we should receive His blessings with joy, but we must also realize that He intends for us to pass those blessings on to future generations. God can use our blessings to open the eyes of jaded, cynical, unbelieving people so that they'll see that He is indeed good.

Heavenly Father, we know that You will bless us as You have promised. Give us the patience to wait for the fulfillment of the blessings. At the same time, we understand that it's not all about us. We need Your wisdom to show us how to pass the blessings on to future generations. In Jesus' name, Amen.

DAY 19

One Portrait, Four Artists

That which was from the beginning, which we have heard, which we have seen with our eyes, which we have looked at and our hands have touched—this we proclaim concerning the Word of life.
1 John 1:2

On an Oxford trip several summers ago, I visited the summer house of Winston Churchill. It was very evident that the rotund Winston Churchill had many sides to his personality. In a picture hanging on the wall, the stern, grim-faced Churchill sits with President Roosevelt. Another portrait shows his more light-hearted side with his family at tea, and there is another picture of him giving the victory sign during World War II. It was the same Winston Churchill, but each painting showed different sides of the man.

That is what you actually see when you read the Gospels. Four biographers are writing about the same subject, yet they highlight different aspects of Jesus. Matthew often draws your attention to Jesus as the teacher. Mark portrays the humanity of Jesus. Luke speaks of Jesus as the one who cares for those who are marginalized, rejected, and dehumanized. John's writing is Christocentric in that every passage points to Christ as the Messiah. Notice that, though each writer emphasizes different aspects of Jesus' character, the subject remains Jesus. Regarding the resurrection, these writers wrote about Jesus and recorded at least seven specific teachings about it over a period of 30 or 40 years, proving the authenticity of this dramatic event. When we share our faith with unbelieving skeptics who doubt that Jesus is alive, we can point them to this incredible truth.

Heavenly Father, we enjoy reading about the different aspects of Jesus' character through the eyes of the four writers of the Gospels. They have provided us with distinctive portraits of our Lord. At the same time, we recognize that our understanding of and relationship with Jesus will continue throughout eternity. We anticipate this with joy. In Jesus' name, Amen.

DAY 20

The New Sabbath Day

On the first day of the week, very early in the morning, the women took the spices they had prepared and went to the tomb.
Luke 24:1

Biblical scholars all agree that the event we call Easter happened on the first day of the week. For today's calendar-makers, this means nothing, but to that ancient world dominated by Rome, it meant everything. The ancient Romans, who were worshipers of the sun, moon, and other assorted gods, named Sunday after the sun, just as they named Saturday after Saturn. But on this day, the whole definition of that day would change. It would be transferred from the dominance of Rome to that small, rejected, abject group of people called Israel. That day, Sunday, would become the new Sabbath, the first day of the week. Indeed, everything would change on that day.

This is the reason why we gather in church on this day. In fact, most devout Christians attend services regularly, but we should not approach this day casually or flippantly. Many of us reduce the Lord's Day to a single hour on Sunday morning. Then, we use the rest of the day to indulge in our own pleasures. However, the Lord has made this whole day unique for His children to worship Him. At the same time, mature Christians know that Resurrection Sunday is not limited to a particular day on the calendar. It is the everyday experience of every believer. Every morning that a believer wakes up and walks in the power of the risen Christ is Resurrection Sunday. Jesus lives! He lives! Let's celebrate every day of the week by giving Him our best in our work, worship, and witness.

REFLECT ON THIS

"Resurrection Sunday is not limited to a particular day on the calendar. It is the everyday experience of every believer. Jesus lives!"

Heavenly Father, we rejoice that every day for us is really Easter. Our very lifestyles should proclaim to a lost and dying world that Jesus lives and moves in the world today. We ask that You conform us into the image of Your Son so that others will be drawn to Him. In Jesus' name, Amen.

DAY 21

Early to Rise

I rise before dawn and cry for help; I have put my hope in your word.
Psalm 119:147

On this first day, the people who came to the tomb arrived very early. It is interesting that one New Testament scholar says that both death and resurrection take place in the darkness. Indeed, there are some things so sacred that even sunlight removes their beauty. On this special morning, death, darkness, and resurrection occurred simultaneously. They both happened on the first day, early in the morning.

In my home church, our sunrise service once began at 4:00 A.M. I asked the pastor at that time, Pastor William Jordan, if they still held sunrise services at the same time. He replied, "You'll be here all by yourself, Ralph."

Jesus got up *early*, *early* – too early for the home church to get up. We should also start our days early. At first light, we should have conversations and fellowship with Jesus. Just as Jesus was the first thought on the minds of the women who visited His tomb early in the morning, He should also be our first thought, not our last. We should meet Him then, not just at night. He should be the beginning of our day. When you face the challenges of the day, you will be glad that you met Jesus early in the morning.

REFLECT ON THIS

*"God should be the beginning
of our day."*

Heavenly Father, we encounter so many challenges on a daily basis that we must start our days with You. As we spend this early time with You, we seek Your wisdom and guidance for the day ahead. We long to hear Your voice in the still quiet of the morning so that we will continue to hear You all day long. In Jesus' name, Amen.

DAY 22

Do You Recognize Jesus?

At this, she turned around and saw Jesus standing there, but she did not realize that it was Jesus.
John 20:14

Most of us have heard stories about celebrities who have been unrecognized in public settings. There have been occasions when well-known personalities have tried to retrieve lost items or conduct everyday business, only to be unrecognized by store employees. When they identify themselves, sometimes the response is skepticism: "I don't care who you say you are." There have been times when we, too, failed to recognize famous people who passed by us. Then a moment of clarity broke through our minds when someone asked, "You know who that was, don't you?"

In the biblical accounts of the resurrection, many people did not recognize the risen Jesus. On at least four occasions, individuals spoke with Jesus, sat with Him, and engaged with Him, yet they failed to recognize who He was because they did not expect Him. At the heart of Easter, over two thousand years ago, no one truly believed Jesus would fulfill what He had promised, which is why they initially missed Him. It was only when Jesus said or did something distinctive that people recognized Him, as when He opened the scriptures and broke bread with the disciples in Luke 24.

Just as the disciples did not recognize Jesus at first, we, too, might overlook His presence during times of grief or uncertainty—moments when it feels as if all hope is lost. Often, we struggle to see Jesus in our circumstances until He speaks to our hearts or does something that only He can do.

When we pause to reflect or pray, we may begin to notice signs of His guidance. We must remember that Jesus promised never to leave us or forsake us. This is the assurance we can offer to a world in need. No matter how lost we feel, recalling Jesus' promise can bring light into our darkest moments. By sharing this assurance with others, we can help them find hope as well.

Heavenly Father, some days are so dark and distressing that we do not recognize You anymore, although You are moving on our behalf. During those times, we cling to that steadfast promise You give to all Your disciples: You will never leave nor forsake us. Open our spiritual eyes so we can recognize You in every situation, no matter how bad it looks on the surface. In Jesus' name, Amen.

DAY 23

No Expectations

"They have taken my Lord away," she said, "and I don't know where they have put him." At this, she turned around and saw Jesus standing there, but she did not realize that it was Jesus.
John 20:13-14

On the first Easter morning at this particular moment, Mary came to view the body. She had come there with perfume to cover up the stench of hopelessness. Future aspirations of a better world had been diminished, and it appeared that the disciples would have to wait even longer for the coming of a Messiah. In her grief, she voices her real pain. She pleads with a man whom she thinks is the gardener, "Where is my Lord? Somebody has come and taken Him. Sir, do you know where they've removed my Lord? Could you please point me in the direction?" What irony! Mary is asking Jesus if He could tell her where He has taken Himself. She did not see Him because she did not expect Him. She assumed somebody had come along and taken His body. But then He called her by name, and she answered, "Rabboni!"— which means teacher.

What a tragedy it would be this Easter to say, "I know Jesus. I have a Bible in my hand, at my house, in my car, and on my iPhone. I grew up in church. I went to Sunday School and the Baptist Training Union. But I do not see Him." You cannot see Him if you are not seeking Him, but when you truly look for Him, you will find Him. God establishes a real and personal relationship with those who earnestly seek Him.

We used to sing as children, "If He calls me, I will answer." When He calls, we must answer. Responding to His call might mean setting aside time for prayer, joining a community of believers, or simply opening your heart and quieting it to listen to His guidance each day. As we respond and draw closer to Him, our relationship with Him grows, and a curious, unsaved world will see something in us that it longs to have.

Heavenly Father, we confess that often we do not recognize You because we are not looking for You. Perhaps we are so afraid You might disappoint us in some way that we do not expect You to show up. Maybe we are avoiding You because we believe You will ask us to do something that we do not want to do. Whatever our excuse, may our hearts be changed so that we are hungry for Your presence. In Jesus' name, Amen.

DAY 24

Fear Not!

The angel said to the women, "Do not be afraid, for I know that you are looking for Jesus, who was crucified.'
Matthew 28:5

B right, shiny, and glistening, an angel perched on top of the stone delivered the Easter message to the women. He began with reassurance, *"Be not afraid."* The women, along with the other disciples to whom the resurrected Jesus appeared later, did not initially recognize Him because of their fear. Because the disciples were not expecting Him, they had buried in the tomb their fears, frustrations, and doubts, but they also buried their betrayals, denials, and unbelief. When Jesus arose on Easter, they figured it out. If He arose, He arose with all the stuff they put in there with Him. Easter was a frightening day for them because if the Lord arose, they had to face all of those negative emotions.

So often we have the same fears regarding our own denials, betrayals, and unbelief. Fortunately, 2 Timothy 1:7 states that, "God has not given us a spirit of fear, but of power, and of love, and of a sound mind." No matter how threatening and powerful the forces of Satan may appear, they are not more powerful than the One who conquered the grave. Today, Jesus says to us, "Stop being scared! Stand up in the power of My resurrection! Face life squarely and believe that all things are possible to him who believes." When we experience the peace of God in the worst situations, unsaved people will marvel and ask why we are not falling apart. We can reply that our Lord has this.

Heavenly Father, so many times our lives are ruled by fear. We're so afraid of the future that we live in a perpetual state of anxiety and stress. The only antidote is to cast ALL our cares and worries upon You. When we simply release them, we will experience peace beyond all understanding. Give us grace and faith to trust You with our fears. In Jesus' name, Amen.

DAY 25

He Lives!

He is not here; he has risen!
Luke 24:6

Every year, tourists fork over plenty of money so they can view the last remains of famous people. Thousands of people fly to Springfield, Illinois, to visit the tomb of Abraham Lincoln. Travelers go to Paris to see Napoleon's tomb or to St. Paul's in London to see the Duke of Wellington. I have been to the Holy Land to see where Jesus was buried. After bending down to get through that little door, I looked around, but no one was there. I asked myself, "What are they coming to look at? They are not coming to find Jesus because He left there on resurrection morning."

He Himself declared it in Revelation 1:18, "I *am* the Living One; I was dead, and now look, I am alive for ever and ever!" No tomb could contain Him then, and no grave will ever hold Him now.

Wherever you go, Christ is already there. He is not in the tomb. He rose, He ascended, and through the Holy Spirit, He is now the constant companion of every believer — here, there, and everywhere. We can confidently echo the words of Alfred Ackley's beloved Easter hymn — He lives, and because He lives, we can face whatever comes. When people ask us, "Why are you always saying that?" we reply, "Because someone is always questioning the reality of who Christ is, but He does not just walk with me and talk with me, He lives in my heart!"

Indeed, Christ Jesus lives today!

Heavenly Father, we find it reassuring that, unlike the founders of other religions, our establisher of the faith is not dead but alive! This is the hope that we proclaim to our unsaved friends and family — that our living Lord can also live inside their hearts. We rejoice that because of Jesus' resurrection, we, too, can live forever! In Jesus' name, Amen.

DAY 26

Jesus Dignifies Women

When Jesus rose early on the first day of the week, he appeared first to Mary Magdalene, out of whom he had driven seven demons.
Mark 16:9

The first witnesses of the resurrection were women, who received the message and promptly went to tell the men. This was important because, in the ancient world, women were treated as nothing, especially if they did not bear sons. They were not allowed to worship with the men. So, you are right when you think the Scriptures appear chauvinistic. That is why you must read past Genesis, Leviticus, Deuteronomy, and the prophets. It was not accidental that of all the people Jesus could have used to tell that message, it was these women. You must know who they were. Some of them had good reputations, but others were rather notorious. The Scriptures remind us that God can use whomever He wants, and He is not asking for permission. When Jesus arose, He dignified these women, granting them the same equality as men at that very moment.

On Easter morning, Jesus Christ dignified all of life by appearing first to women. Some of these women had good reputations, while others had rather notorious pasts. Mary Magdalene herself had been delivered from seven demons. Yet Jesus trusted them with the most important news in human history. 'He is risen!' The Lord elevated these women to a position of honor and equality, giving them a voice and a mission.

This was not just about elevating women; it was about Jesus dignifying all people. He came to restore value to everyone the world had discarded, rejected, or deemed worthless. On resurrection morning, Jesus demonstrated that in God's kingdom, everyone matters. Everyone has worth. Everyone has a voice. Everyone can be a witness.

Heavenly Father, we hope women find comfort in knowing they don't have to compete for equal attention in Your kingdom. You value women, as shown through Your Son Jesus. Keep working through us to reach women whom society has dismissed as worthless. It is a joy to serve as tools of restoration in their lives. In Jesus' name, Amen.

DAY 27

Go Tell Somebody!

Then go quickly and tell his disciples: He has risen from the dead and is going ahead of you into Galilee. There you will see him.' Now I have told you."
Matthew 28:7

At work, at home, and at play, can you do what Jesus told the women to do? *Go tell somebody.* That is Easter. If you miss that point, you miss its true meaning. Go tell somebody! Whom do we tell? The angel said, "Go tell Peter," who represents all kinds of people, young and old, those who are up and those who are down, male and female, the haves and the have-nots. Go tell Peter or go tell Katrina—it doesn't matter who it is; just go tell somebody that Jesus is alive. That is the real message of Easter. After everything else, go tell somebody.

Unfortunately, so many of us have heard today's news so often that it no longer shocks or surprises us. Yet I still find myself surprised and overwhelmed by it. I understand, though, when you know a lot about a subject, you might think there is nothing left to learn. Some say, "You can tell me about Jesus, but I know everything." I've heard that before, and I always reply, "That's amazing. Every week, I am still trying to figure it out, still trying to learn, still trying to grow." Every week when I come to church, I do not wait for a special day to share the gospel. For me, every day is Resurrection Sunday, and the news is too good to keep to myself. I must tell somebody that Jesus lives!

Heavenly Father, it is our joyful privilege and honor to share the gospel with those who don't know Your Son. Refresh our hearts and minds so that we'll never grow complacent or lackadaisical regarding its life-transforming power. Place a burning desire within us to tell everyone that You're alive! In Jesus' name, Amen.

DAY 28

If You See Something, Say Something

"As for us, we cannot help speaking about what we have seen and heard."
Acts 4:20

In New York City, many years ago, a wannabe bomber parked his car, rigged with explosives, in a busy area. Fortunately, alert bystanders noticed something suspicious and alerted authorities. The bomb did not detonate, and they found the bomber. The police dismantled the bomb. Likewise, following the September 11 attacks, officials became increasingly concerned about public safety and potential threats in crowded places and launched a campaign with the motto, 'If you see something, you should say something.' They informed the public, "If you see a bag on a train or at the cab stand that's left unattended or something doesn't feel right, just say something."

These authorities may not have been Christians, but they urged people to share important tips to keep others safe.

As believers, we have the best news in the world that can save others—the life-changing gospel of Jesus Christ. When the Lord has been good to us, we should say something. Nobody should have to urge us to share what God has done.

If we knew the Lord woke us up, watched over us, and started us on our way, we should say something. When we must travel safely from place to place under God's protection, we should say something because we have seen His goodness. In a world flooded with bad news, accidents, problems, and break-ins, it is refreshing to testify that the Lord has kept us safe from disasters because He is good. If God has been good to you, you should say so.

Heavenly Father, the authorities in our society have heightened our awareness of potential threats to our safety to the point that we will report anything suspicious we see, even if we are not sure. But we know what we've seen and heard regarding the gospel of Jesus Christ. It would be a crime of a spiritual kind not to share what we KNOW to be true. Give us the same kind of urgency to convey this lifesaving news. In Jesus' name, Amen.

DAY 29

Just the Facts

After his suffering, he presented himself to them and gave many convincing proofs that he was alive.
Acts 1:3

Some of you may remember the 1960s television police drama "Dragnet" about a pair of Los Angeles detectives who solved crimes each week. When Joe Friday was investigating crimes and gathering evidence, he would often say to a potential witness, "Just the facts — just the facts." Friday knew that random speculation was not enough, he needed solid evidence to bring the guilty party to justice, and evidence demands a verdict.

As Christians living in a skeptical world, we will be asked why we believe in Jesus Christ. If we commit the first four verses of 1 Corinthians 15 to memory, we can confidently respond, "I believe according to the Scriptures." When they press further with "How do you believe this?", we can answer, "There are eyewitness accounts that have faithfully passed this truth down through the generations." As we examine the four Gospel accounts of the resurrection, written by four different people at four different times, our faith is renewed and strengthened by their corresponding testimonies. No one gathered these four writers in a room and told them what to say. They wrote independently, at different times, and still arrived at the same extraordinary conclusion.

We do not celebrate the resurrection merely because it is a cherished tradition. We celebrate because we believe in the facts that Jesus Christ died for our sins, was buried, and on the third day rose again exactly as the Scriptures promised. That is not speculation. That is the verdict the evidence demands!

Heavenly Father, we're thankful that we not only have experiential evidence that Jesus is alive, but there are also plenty of factual proofs to back up this actual historical event. When skeptics question us about the validity of the resurrection, bring all these facts to our remembrance to share with them. In Jesus' name, Amen.

DAY 30

Jesus' Personal Appearances— Inside and Outside

After that, he appeared to more than five hundred of the brothers and sisters at the same time, most of whom are still living, though some have fallen asleep.
1 Corinthians 15:6

To prove that He rose from the dead that first Easter morning, Jesus appeared to individual people outdoors and indoors. Over the years, skeptics have dismissed the resurrection as a fallacy, claiming that the body of Christ was stolen by the brokenhearted disciples before His placement in the tomb. However, the truth, according to the Scriptures, is that Jesus died for our sins and was buried, but He arose and appeared outside the tomb to Mary Magdalene and other women. The risen Christ also appeared inside to His disciples gathered in the upper room. While they were there, He provided tangible evidence to prove that He was not a ghost and that they were not hallucinating. Jesus told Thomas to examine His hands and side so he would know for himself that He was real. He then ate fish in their presence to prove that He was indeed alive. But Jesus did not just appear to individuals; He also appeared to large groups, totaling approximately 500.

Why do we talk about these appearances? It is because there is no discrepancy between the eyewitness reports. All the people testified that they saw Him in Jerusalem and Galilee. He was in the capital city, Jerusalem, walking through the marketplace, where His followers would be able to identify Him. Today, although we are not direct eyewitnesses to His resurrection, we see clear evidence of His work in our own lives that proves to us He is alive and well.

Heavenly Father, Jesus appeared to many people after His resurrection, demonstrating in many ways that He was not a ghost or a hallucination. We are thankful that He has also appeared in our lives in such powerful ways that we know He is very alive and well. As we share our experience, we prepare the hearts of others by melting away their skepticism and unbelief. In Jesus' name, Amen.

DAY 31

Here, There, and Everywhere

Where can I go from your Spirit? Where can I flee from your presence?
Psalm 139:7

In the height of life's experiences, Christ can be there, and in the low places of life, He can be there, too. David understood this intimately when he wrote in Psalm 139, "If I go up to the heavens, you are there; if I make my bed in the depths, you are there. If I rise on the wings of the dawn, if I settle on the far side of the sea, even there your hand will guide me." There is no place that is off-limits to where Christ can be — not in your highest moment of celebration, not in your deepest valley of despair, not at the dawn of a new beginning, not in the farthest place you could ever run. He can come and assist you here and there, not just in Jerusalem and Galilee, not just to individuals and groups, not just indoors and outdoors, but here and now.

Christ can appear in different places at the same time — here, there, and everywhere. In His earthly ministry, He was limited to one place. He had to die and be resurrected so He could be everywhere at once.

In His final words to the disciples, He made this promise to every believer in Matthew 28:20, "And surely I am with you always, to the very end of the age." That promise was not just for the disciples; it was for every person who would ever place their faith in Him.

In the daylight, He arose, and the angels testified by asking the women, "Why are you looking for the living among the dead?" That is why a church can never reach cemetery status. This is no mausoleum or museum. We are the body of Jesus, who is our Head, ministering the good news of the gospel to our world. We come to serve a resurrected Christ, a living Christ, a living Lord. We come to worship Christ Himself, the Living Lord who is here, there, and everywhere.

REFLECT ON THIS

*"The Living Lord is here,
there, and everywhere — and
He is with you."*

Heavenly Father, we are comforted by the fact that Jesus is available here, there, and everywhere. We do not have to worry that He is not around when we need Him. Since He is alive, we who are believers are alive in Him and always will be. Remind us of this truth when we feel like giving up. In Jesus' name, Amen.

DAY 32

The Road to Emmaus

As they talked and discussed these things with each other, Jesus himself came up and walked along with them.
Luke 24:15

In this account, Jesus has already been resurrected. Now we join up with Cleopas and his nameless companion walking to the suburbs of Emmaus. Seven miles outside Jerusalem, they are discussing in detail what took place from Friday to this day. The conclusion these two followers of Jesus have reached is that the Promised One who died on the cross cannot be who He claims to be. So, they are walking into the sunset of disappointment. As they're walking, suddenly they're joined by a stranger. These travelers now have a companion. Luke says that God seized their eyes. The word "seized" indicates that God Himself prevented them from recognizing Jesus. They were so preoccupied with their disappointment and personal pain that they started believing that Easter was about them and not about God.

We must ensure we do not miss the reality of Easter because we are preoccupied with disappointments on our road to Emmaus. Some of us are disappointed today because our jobs drain us, or we are struggling in our marriages. We are disappointed because we are looking at life through narrow slits. Yet today, God can take your disappointments and give you a clarity of vision to see home, life, and work from His perspective of fulfillment in Christ alone. Indeed, you can only find wholeness in the Lord Jesus Christ, and it's only when you are whole that you can be a help to somebody else.

Heavenly Father, we confess that the disappointments in our lives have seriously clouded our vision to the point that we are unable to recognize You. We pray that You will give us spiritual eyes to see You clearly once again, so that we can minister effectively to others. In Jesus' name, Amen.

DAY 33

He's Everything to Me

And my God will meet all your needs according to the riches of his glory in Christ Jesus.
Philippians 4:19

The mysterious stranger on the road to Emmaus—who was really Jesus—told the travelers, "These things had to take place for the Scriptures to be fulfilled." He was actually describing Himself, starting with the books written by Moses. He says in Genesis that He is the sea; in Exodus, He's a deliverer. In Numbers, He's the lifted circle; in Deuteronomy, He's the living word. In Joshua, He's a battle axe; in Judges, He's the Lord who shall come; in Kings and Chronicles, and in Samuel, He is the King of Kings and Lord of Lords. Then He discussed what the prophets said about Him. He says now in Isaiah, He's the Prince of Peace; in Jeremiah, He's the balm in Gilead. Then He declares that in Daniel, He's a stone hewed out of a mountain, tearing the wonders of Babylon down. In Hosea, He is love; in Micah, He is mercy; and in David's writing, He is music.

Jesus, who is the same yesterday, today, and forever, is the culmination of all these characteristics. He completely fulfills every single prophecy written in the Torah and the books of the prophets as the Lamb of God who takes away the sin of the world. As those who have been cleansed by His blood, we have the joyous privilege and responsibility to tell others that He can be everything for them as well.

REFLECT ON THIS

*"Jesus completely fulfills
every single prophecy as the
Lamb of God who takes away
the sin of the world."*

Heavenly Father, we rejoice that Jesus indeed is everything to us—Savior, Deliverer, Wonderful Counselor, the Prince of Peace, and so much more. Because of this assurance, no situation is too difficult, and no obstacle is impossible to overcome. When others ask us the reason for the hope that is in us, help us to readily give them the Answer: Jesus!! In Jesus' name, Amen.

DAY 34

Stay with Us, Lord!

But they urged him strongly, "Stay with us, for it is nearly evening; the day is almost over." So he went in to stay with them.
Luke 24:29

On that dusty road to Emmaus, the stranger kept on talking. When the travelers reached their house, the Gospel writer Luke said, "He acted like he would keep on going." When Jesus talked to these disciples along the way, they pleaded with Him, "Don't keep walking. Come home with us." They discovered that when they invited Him in, He initially responded as a guest, but once He walked across the threshold, He became *the host.* They had been walking all day, so He most likely washed their feet and hands. After they said grace, He took over and served them bread.

At some point in your life, you must ask the Lord to stay with you because He is always on the move. Jesus always has somewhere to go, so you must ask Him, "Lord, will You stay here with me?" He will never turn down that invitation. When He takes over, He brings order to chaos, peace to anxiety, and clarity to confusion. The disciples on the road to Emmaus discovered this firsthand — what began as a conversation with a stranger ended with their hearts burning within them. Just realize that every time you invite Him in, He will take over the circumstance, and the next thing you know, you will see something.

REFLECT ON THIS

*"Every time you invite Him in,
He will take over the
circumstance."*

Heavenly Father, we do not want Jesus to just be a visiting guest in our hearts and lives; instead, we want Him to be the only permanent resident. We surrender every place in our hearts that we have closed to Him in the past. Jesus, come and make Your home in us! In Jesus' name, Amen.

DAY 35

The Broken

When he was at the table with them, he took bread, gave thanks, broke it, and began to give it to them. Then their eyes were opened, and they recognized him, and he disappeared from their sight.
Luke 24:30-31

Jesus took the bread, blessed it, and then broke it. The travelers thought to themselves, *That looks familiar. Wait a minute; I've seen this before.* They looked at each other as He gave the bread to them, and when they recognized *those hands* that had broken and blessed, *those hands* that had been nailed, *those hands*, they thought, *Those are—well, we know who this is. This is not a stranger. This is the one that hung on the cross! He got up, and now he is at our house.* They could not eat. After Jesus suddenly vanished, they said to each other, *didn't our hearts burn within as He talked with us along the way?*

That is what this post-resurrection event reminds us—that the same God on the other side of resurrection who took us, blessed us, broke us, and gave us away now in resurrection will come into our lives and use them if we just give them to Him. When He comes into our lives, He will bless them, but we must always realize that breaking precedes blessing. For

God to get the best out of us, He must break us first. Sometimes He breaks us when we deliberately go our own way and sin, but other times, He breaks us with trials of His own making. Nevertheless, all of us who follow Christ will get broken. It is only then that He can give us away to people in our families, neighborhoods, workplaces, and churches. Yes, He will! He will give us away so that we can help others.

Heavenly Father, we realize that just like the bread, we must be broken before You can give us away to a spiritually starving world. Give us the grace to endure the trials with patience, and then, when we are ready to minister, stoke our desire to minister to others. In Jesus' name, Amen.

DAY 36

Only One Perfect Somebody

And let us consider how we may spur one another on toward love and good deeds, not giving up meeting together, as some are in the habit of doing, but encouraging one another—and all the more as you see the Day approaching.
Hebrews 10:24-25

D
o not miss God because of disappointment. Do not allow death, grief, hate, bitterness, and unfulfilled dreams keep you from seeing God. Instead, let God seize your eyes so that you will see what He wants you to see. He calls us to gather in the community of faith to support each other in times of disappointment. That is the answer to this whole dilemma for these disciples. My heart breaks when I see Christians abandon the church or lose focus on the significance and work of the fellowship.

Sometimes I hear church members saying, "I'm looking for perfect people." They get upset when they see broken and fragmented folks in the fellowship, so they walk away from the church, disillusioned because their perceptions are shattered. In all my years of walking with the Lord, I have never gone to church looking for perfect people. When I was a young Christian in my teens, I knew there was only one perfect person, and that was the Lord Jesus Christ. That's why I come to church—people who are imperfect, broken, shattered, lost, and confused can come into the fellowship to meet others who are broken, shattered, and confused. The good news is that we do not have to stay that way. We can show our brokenness to somebody else who will say, "Yeah, you're broken, but God knows how to put you back together again." Oh, yes, He will, and He accomplishes that feat through the intense pressures of life.

Heavenly Father, we thank You for the security and protection that Your church provides to every believer. Forgive us when we allow bitterness and disillusionment to keep us from the fellowship. We need each other! Also, we realize that You are the only perfect one. Give us the grace to forgive others when they hurt us. In Jesus' name, Amen.

DAY 37

The Church on Fire

See, I have refined you, though not as silver; I have tested you in the furnace of affliction.
Isaiah 48:10

M onterey pine trees that grow in California have pine cones that remain tightly closed, sealed in resin. Nothing can force these cones to open—not hammers, not tools, nothing. They open only when exposed to intense heat from fire. When a forest fire moves through, the heat melts away the resin, the cones open, and the seeds fall to the ground.

The church is like that. We gather as broken people who have been through the fire trials, disappointments, and suffering. It is in the heat of life's pressures that we open and share our struggles with one another. The church is not filled with perfect people who have never faced difficulties. It is a place where people have experienced the refining fire of God's work in their lives. In fellowship, we open our hearts to one another, and new spiritual life develops. Churches where people pray for you, encourage you, and walk with you through the hours of life are beautiful because we are all being refined together.

Often, we want to attend a church that does not have many people under fire. We look for a place where everyone appears perfect. But we must go where people have been forgiven of their sins and found in their lostness. It is there, in true fellowship, that we open up and new life develops. Church is a good place—but you cannot truly love church if you keep God on a schedule. If you only pencil God into your calendar when it is convenient, you do not understand church. You do not attend church; you *are* the church. Church is where people come to pray for you. We must be careful not to become so perfectionistic or legalistic that we require people to meet a certain standard before they belong.
criteria.

Heavenly Father, we know the church is as vital to believers as breathing. Despite the pain we're going through, we're going to joyfully gather together with other brothers and sisters in the faith for support and encouragement. Forgive us when we avoid church because it is inconvenient or because we feel the people there do not meet our "standard." Remind us often that we are not perfect, just forgiven! In Jesus' name, Amen.

DAY 38

Gone AWOL

"I'm going out to fish," Simon Peter told them, and they said,
"We'll go with you."
John 21:3

In John 21, the disciples knew all too well that Jesus had been resurrected. In the previous chapter, Jesus instructed Mary Magdalene to tell His disciples and Peter that He was alive. Yet seven of the eleven disciples decided to resume their occupation as fishermen. Even though they had once followed Him and had heard the message about His resurrection, they chose to return to what they had done before Jesus called them. In the morning by the seaside, Jesus appeared and saw them fishing. The resurrected Lord was present, so it was time to re-engage in their discipleship activity, but they were absent without leave (AWOL) at that moment. He wanted to see what kept them so preoccupied that they could stay away from where they were supposed to be for so long. They did not recognize Him because they were running in the wrong direction. Somehow, they were blinded because they were not seeing Him for who He was.

Perhaps, just like the disciples, you have expected Jesus to do something for you or to be something else altogether, and you feel that He has let you down. Out of anger, frustration, and disappointment, you may have gone AWOL (absent without leave) from your active service to the Lord in His church, choosing instead to engage in familiar, seemingly "good" worldly activities. However, you must realize that no matter what you think would be good for your life, God always has the best in mind for you. That is where trust and obedience become essential. When you acknowledge Jesus as the Lord of your life, you must do what He expects of you—not the other way around.

Heavenly Father, in Your gracious mercy, You are calling us from our AWOL status back into Your service. Forgive us for backsliding into the easy coziness of the world because the going got tough. We know that You truly know what is best for us in all aspects of our lives. In Jesus' name, Amen.

DAY 39

Fishing on the Wrong Side of the Boat

He said, "Throw your net on the right side of the boat, and you will find some." When they did, they were unable to haul the net in because of the large number of fish.
John 21:6

O nce again, just as in Luke 5, the disciples were doing the same thing—fishing from the wrong side of the boat. Jesus must have been shaking His head as He told them, "Do you not know by now that you will never be successful without Me? You are simply spinning your wheels and running in circles." The first thing Jesus said was, "Let your nets down on the right side of the boat." They were in the same water, on the same lake. The only difference was the side of the boat. Why could they not catch fish on one side instead of the other? It was because one side was the wrong side and the other was the right one. When Jesus said, "Let your nets down," they immediately obeyed Him because He is the Lord.

I have seen rich people who have all kinds of fancy titles and prestige, but they are restless all the time. They never have any joy because nothing is ever good enough. As a result, they are always looking for something else to fulfill their lives. But anytime Jesus is not involved in your life, you are living on the wrong side of the boat, and nothing good will ever come out of your life. If you come and live on the right side, however, you will find joy, excitement, love, peace, and power. Experiencing the Lord's powerful work in your life naturally leads to sharing that transformation with your unsaved friends and family, just as these disciples did. After all, there is nothing more persuasive than a transformed life.

REFLECT ON THIS

*"There is nothing more
persuasive than a
transformed life."*

Heavenly Father, we confess that we have wasted precious time living on the wrong side of the boat. We have pursued earthly pleasures and material things while paying You lip service for a couple of hours in church every Sunday. We repent, Lord, and ask You to forgive us for our waywardness. Give us empowering grace to live for You on the right side of the boat. In Jesus' name, Amen.

DAY 40

The Commission of Easter

"But go, tell his disciples and Peter, 'He is going ahead of you into Galilee. There you will see him, just as he told you.'"
Mark 16:7

The real message of Easter is simply this: "Go tell Peter and the other disciples to meet Him in Galilee." Now, when the angel delivered this message from Jesus, it carried weight. In other words, the Lord says through the angel, "Peter has jettisoned the faith. He is on the wrong trajectory because he thinks I can no longer use him. I know he lied when he said he did not know Me but go get Peter because I can use him. I have a book that I need him to write. He has not always been wrong. He did say I was the Christ, the Son of the Living God. So, go get Peter and bring him with you to Galilee, where I will meet you."

The visitors comprehended the angel's underlying message: A dead man does not tell you to meet him somewhere. He was actually saying, "Tell them Jesus is not dead, but alive."

The true commission of Easter is to tell people news that is too good to keep to yourself. If people have really received the gospel message personally, they will talk about it. Christians can talk in church about how much they love Jesus all they want, but if they are not telling unsaved people about it, they have never really tasted it. As His followers, we must keep telling people the old, old story over and over again.

Heavenly Father, we realize that the commission of Easter is quite simple—to proclaim the gospel to every living creature. We indeed have good news to tell! Give us the boldness and faith to tell others about the salvation that Jesus offers through His sacrificial death on the cross and glorious resurrection. We look forward to seeing many people added to Your kingdom. In Jesus' name, Amen.

ABIDE IN HIS PRESENCE

A Closing Meditation

You have walked forty days with the Lord through this devotional. You have traveled from the Triumphal Entry to the empty tomb, from Palm Sunday to Resurrection Sunday, from the crowds lining the streets of Jerusalem to the disciples fishing on the wrong side of the boat. Along the way, you have been challenged to proclaim the gospel and praise the God who makes all things new.

The journey does not end here. Abiding in Christ is a lifetime commitment. David understood this. In every season of his life, whether he was running from his enemies or sitting on the throne of Israel, he kept coming back to the same conviction: he wanted to dwell in the house of the Lord. That is the heartbeat of Psalm 27.

Read it slowly. Read it again. Let these words become your own as you move forward from this Lenten season into the everyday life of a follower of Jesus Christ.

PSALM 27
Of David.

1 The Lord is my light and my salvation—
whom shall I fear?
The Lord is the stronghold of my life—
of whom shall I be afraid?

2 When the wicked advance against me
to devour[a] me,
it is my enemies and my foes
who will stumble and fall.
3 Though an army besiege me,
my heart will not fear;
though war break out against me,
even then I will be confident.

4 One thing I ask from the Lord,
this only do I seek:
that I may dwell in the house of the Lord
all the days of my life,
to gaze on the beauty of the Lord

and to seek him in his temple.

5 For in the day of trouble
he will keep me safe in his dwelling;
he will hide me in the shelter of his sacred tent
and set me high upon a rock.

6 Then my head will be exalted
above the enemies who surround me;
at his sacred tent I will sacrifice with shouts of joy;
I will sing and make music to the Lord.

7 Hear my voice when I call, Lord;
be merciful to me and answer me.
8 My heart says of you, "Seek his face!"
Your face, Lord, I will seek.
9 Do not hide your face from me,
do not turn your servant away in anger;
you have been my helper.
Do not reject me or forsake me,
God my Savior.
10 Though my father and mother forsake me,
the Lord will receive me.
11 Teach me your way, Lord;
lead me in a straight path

because of my oppressors.

12 Do not turn me over to the desire of my foes,

for false witnesses rise up against me,

spouting malicious accusations.

13 I remain confident of this:

I will see the goodness of the Lord

in the land of the living.

14 Wait for the Lord;

be strong and take heart

and wait for the Lord.

Forty days ago, you began this journey. Today you continue it. Proclaim what you know to be true. Praise the God who brought you through. And keep seeking His face because that is what abiding looks like in real life, every single day.

Seek His face. Always.

Be Encouraged.

Ralph Douglas West Ministries

ADDITIONAL TITLES BY RALPH DOUGLAS WEST

- *Pas the Day: 365 Daily Devotional Journal*
- *Finding Fullness Again: What the Book of Ruth Teaches us about Starting Over*
- *Left Alone: Finding Strength for Life's Mysteries, Impossibilities, and Uncertainties*
- *Living in the In-Between Times: The Life of Samuel*
- *An Uplook for a New Outlook: 30 Days to a New View*
- *Forget Not: 21 Days to Discover the Power of Daily Gratitude*
- *The Prince with Four Names: Daily Devotional for Advent*
- *Boomerang* (available March 17, 2026)

ABOUT THE AUTHOR

Ralph Douglas West, affectionately known as "Pas," is the Founder and Pastor of The Church Without Walls in Houston, Texas, where he has served for almost four decades. A pastor, scholar, teacher, and great orator, he has been named one of the *12 Most Effective Preachers in the English-Speaking World* by Baylor University's Truett Theological Seminary and among the *40 Most Influential Preachers of the Past 40 Years* by *Preaching Magazine.*

Pastor West's ministry extends beyond the pulpit through leadership development, community engagement, and a heart for justice and reconciliation. His preaching combines theological depth with practical application, speaking to contemporary issues while remaining firmly rooted in Scripture. Known for his profound biblical insights and passionate delivery, Pastor West is committed to building a diverse, inclusive community of faith.

Recognized worldwide for his expository preaching, he teaches at Truett Seminary and has spoken at Oxford University and the Baptist World Congress.

For more messages and resources from
Pastor Ralph Douglas West,
visit www.ralphdouglaswest.com.

Pas

RALPH DOUGLAS WEST
MINISTRIES

100